HOMES
IN MY LIFETIME

Written by
Rebecca Phillips-Bartlett

American adaptation copyright © 2026 by North Star Editions, Mendota Heights, MN 55120. All rights reserved. No part of this book may be reproduced or utilized in any form or by any means without written permission from the publisher.

Homes © 2024 BookLife Publishing
This edition is published by arrangement with BookLife Publishing

sales@northstareditions.com
888-417-0195

Library of Congress Control Number:
2025930422

ISBN
979-8-89359-324-2 (library bound)
979-8-89359-408-9 (paperback)
979-8-89359-380-8 (epub)
979-8-89359-354-9 (hosted ebook)

Printed in the United States of America
Mankato, MN
092025

Written by:
Rebecca Phillips-Bartlett

Edited by:
Alex Hall

Designed by:
Jasmine Pointer

All facts, statistics, web addresses and URLs in this book were verified as valid and accurate at time of writing. No responsibility for any changes to external websites or references can be accepted by either the author or publisher.

Image Credits

Images courtesy of Shutterstock.com, unless otherwise stated.

Cover – ilikeyellow, PaintDoor, Sasha Mosyagina, RinaArt21, Andrew Rybalko. Throughout – Andrew Rybalko. 6–7 – Roadblocknine, CC BY-SA 4.0 <https://creativecommons.org/licenses/by-sa/4.0/>, via Wikimedia Commons, Stokkete, Hannes Grobe, CC BY-SA 4.0 <https://creativecommons.org/licenses/by-sa/4.0/>, via Wikimedia Commons, sherilhome_sherilhouse. 8–9 – NotarYES, NASA, Public domain, via Wikimedia Commons, Kseniia Gorova. 10–11 – rafa jodar, Kartinkin77, Zuktenvos, DAMRONG RATTANAPONG, Ribkhan, Ned Snowman, Solonesafe. 12–13 – Ursula Page, Go My Media, WianggaNelwand. 14–15 – Lushchikov Valeriy. 16–17 – LIAL, Prostock-studio, DrMadra, balabolka, katsumatakun. 18–19 – Hazal Ak, Tero Vesalainen, Giuliano Del Moretto, jennyt, Triff, New Africa. 22–23 – IGORdeyka, Tenstudio, Vectorbum.

CONTENTS

Page 4 Back in My Day
Page 6 When I Was Born
Page 8 When I Was Young
Page 12 I Remember...
Page 16 How Very Modern!
Page 18 Nowadays...
Page 20 Nana's Timeline
Page 22 Tomorrow's World
Page 24 Glossary and Index

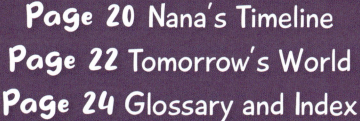

Words that look like <u>this</u> can be found in the glossary on page 24.

BACK IN MY DAY

Mom! Nana Pam is here!

Mom and Layla were busy building <u>flat-pack furniture</u>. Suddenly, the doorbell rang. Mom stopped what she was doing. She let Nana Pam in. The floor was cluttered with tools. The instruction video was paused on the TV.

WHEN I WAS BORN

Before Nana was born in 1959, her dad learned how to do <u>carpentry</u>. He learned how to build wooden furniture. He used everything he learned to build Nana's crib.

Flat-pack furniture was not common back then. They didn't need step-by-step instructions. Instead, they came up with their own plans. Many power tools had not been <u>invented</u> yet. They did a lot of work by hand.

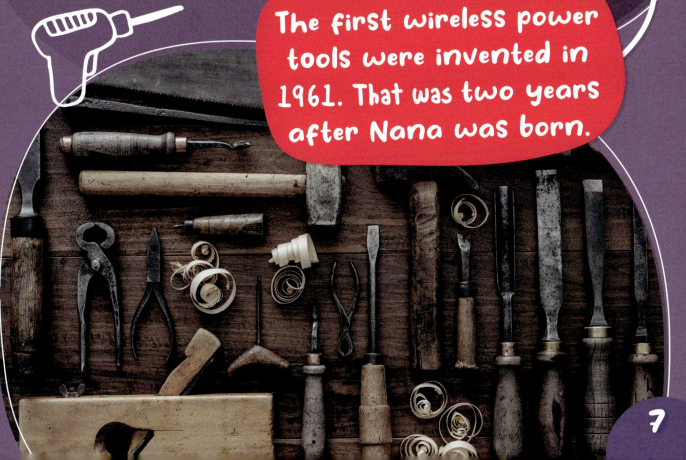

The first wireless power tools were invented in 1961. That was two years after Nana was born.

WHEN I WAS YOUNG

When Nana was little, there were only a few TV channels. Everything on TV was in black and white. Grown-ups learned about important events by watching them on TV.

In the 1970s, Nana listened to rock music on cassette tapes. Her parents listened to classical music on vinyl records.

The problem was that cassette and record players were big. That all changed when the Walkman was invented in 1979. The Walkman was one of the first personal music players.

I could plug in my headphones and take my Walkman wherever I went!

I REMEMBER...

"In 1982, Gramps and I got married. We bought our first house that year, too."

Nana and Gramps were given lots of wedding presents, such as plates, saucepans, and mixers. These helped them get started in their new home. Their house was very different than their childhood homes.

One of the biggest differences was the kitchen. Nana and Gramps' kitchen had many new gadgets. In 1986, they got their first microwave.

Your mom and aunt had just been born. The microwave was very helpful to heat up food quickly!

Percy Spencer

The microwave oven was invented by mistake. In 1945, a scientist called Percy Spencer was <u>experimenting</u> with something called radar.

14

One day, he was standing next to his machine. He noticed that the candy bar in his pocket melted. He quickly realized this machine could be used to heat up food. Soon, he was snacking on the world's first microwave popcorn.

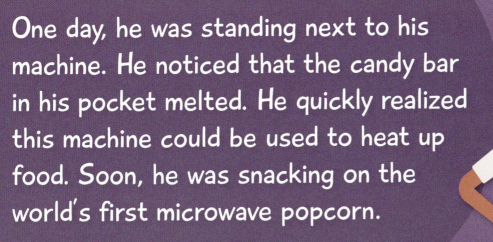

Let's make our own popcorn!

HOW VERY MODERN!

Mom and Nana got their first DVD player in 2001. At the time, DVDs felt very modern! Before that, they watched movies on VHS tapes.

16

NOWADAYS...

Nowadays, there are all sorts of <u>devices</u> that make life easier in many ways.

Air fryer

Microwaves, slow cookers, and air fryers make cooking food easier than ever.

People can watch videos and find information at the click of a button on TVs, phones, and tablets.

However, lots of older inventions are still important today!

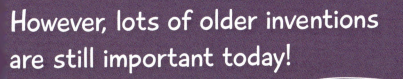

Door locks were invented thousands of years ago. They still keep us safe today.

Books are a very old invention. They are still a great way to explore stories and learn about the world.

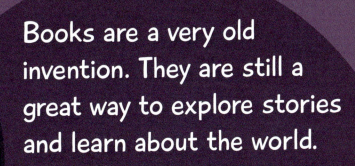

19

NANA'S TIMELINE

"Homes have changed a lot in my lifetime. Let's look back at my timeline."

1969—Nana watched the moon landing on a black and white TV.

1970s—Nana listened to music on cassette tapes.

1961—Wireless tools were invented.

1959—Nana was born.

1979—The Walkman was invented.

1980s—Nana watched movies on VHS tapes.

1982—Nana and Gramps got married and bought a house.

1985—Mom and Auntie Jo were born.

1986—Nana got a microwave.

2001—Nana got a DVD player.

21

TOMORROW'S WORLD

Lots of brand-new inventions are created all the time. Many inventions are made to solve problems or help people.

Is there anything you do around the house that could be made easier? What could you invent to solve that problem?

What would YOU invent?

GLOSSARY

carpentry	making and fixing things using wood
devices	machines or inventions made to do something
experimenting	doing tests to see what happens
flat-pack furniture	furniture that is bought in many pieces and put together at home
invented	when something new is created for the first time
modern	to do with recent or present times
personal	belongs to one person rather than anyone else
stream	to receive information over the internet, such as videos or shows

INDEX

books 19
DVD players 16, 21
furniture 4, 6–7
kitchens 13
microwaves 13–15, 18, 21
moon 9, 20
movies 16–17, 21

music 10–11, 20
popcorn 15–16
tapes 10, 16–17, 20–21
tools 4, 7, 20
TVs 4, 8, 18, 20
weddings 12